**Follow this recipe and you will
have a winning story!**

Ingredients you will need:

2 cups of passion

1 cup of purpose

A tablespoonful of inspiration

A pinch of discipline

A bowlful of memories

Passion To Paper

A Simple Recipe for Writing
Your Personal Story

By Sherree A. Felstead

BALBOA
PRESS

A DIVISION OF HAY HOUSE

Balboa Press books may be ordered through booksellers or by contacting:

Balboa Press
A Division of Hay House
1663 Liberty Drive
Bloomington, IN 47403
www.balboapress.com
1-(877) 407-4847

Because of the dynamic nature of the Internet, any web addresses or links contained in this book may have changed since publication and may no longer be valid. The views expressed in this work are solely those of the author and do not necessarily reflect the views of the publisher, and the publisher hereby disclaims any responsibility for them.

The author of this book does not dispense medical advice or prescribe the use of any technique as a form of treatment for physical, emotional, or medical problems without the advice of a physician, either directly or indirectly. The intent of the author is only to offer information of a general nature to help you in your quest for emotional and spiritual well-being. In the event you use any of the information in this book for yourself, which is your constitutional right, the author and the publisher assume no responsibility for your actions.

Any people depicted in stock imagery provided by Thinkstock are models, and such images are being used for illustrative purposes only.
Certain stock imagery © Thinkstock.

ISBN: 978-1-4525-7079-2 (sc)
ISBN: 978-1-4525-7080-8 (e)

Printed in the United States of America.

Balboa Press rev. date: 03/14/2014

For more information, contact passiontopaper @bell.net
Website: www.passiontopaper.ca
Written by Sherree A. Felstead
Graphic Design by Lillian Jia
Art Illustration by Matt Hoffman
Author Photo by Kelly Taylor Photography.

Author's Message

How often do we sit back and reflect on the story that we've played the principal role in? We sometimes live tough, enduring lives bursting with joy and feeling for all we have done. Yet, we tend to assume that other people's lives or talents make better stories than our own. We yearn for their experience and live vicariously through them, when in fact we are full of our own amazing experiences. We only need to uncover and express them.

One of the few things that provide a sense of continuity in these fractured times is the story. Historians and archaeologists have uncovered many stories written about humankind. Some were written on stone tablets, while others were drawn on cave walls or erected as monuments. However, the stories of our forebearers are one thing, but what about our own?

Isn't it time to set our ideas, experiences and sentiments down so others can benefit? By telling our story, we not only validate our existence, but clarify the vision of ourselves. This kind of internal connection is hard to match.

So often when people write their story, they are taken aback by what they read on the page: their accomplishments, failures, sense of wonder, even their own humanity. Telling their story either nurtured and nourished them or led them to lead more fulfilling lives. The beauty of recording our stories is that we are self-fulfilled.

I've been helping people write their stories for many years. Some of them have been published in magazines and books. Others were more for personal gratification.

My book, ***Passion to Paper: A simple recipe for writing your personal story*** is the perfect primer to get you started. Throughout the book, there are exercises that open new doorways to the creative self, and practical steps to bring your story to life on the page; information on how to publish (if you chose to do so), and 'expressions' from famous writers that provide insights and encouragement.

I hope you enjoy using the book and that your journey to putting your passion on to paper is enlightening.

Dedication

This book is dedicated to the employees and peers I've worked with throughout my career as a professional communicator. It was my pleasure to help you bring your stories to life, whether it was a speech, an article, a presentation or a book. You made me see the immeasurable value in what I do. It brought me the greatest satisfaction to see your faces light up when you read your own story. The pleasure was all mine.

However, I cannot forget family, friends or acquaintances who verbally shared their personal stories with me over a cup of coffee, on the street or at a gathering of some sort.

As a friend or colleague, all of you made me realize there is a need for people to find a way to tell their stories, without the angst the writing process often creates. So often I've heard, *"I'm not a writer; I hate writing or if I have to write my story, I can't do it."* I perfectly understand how you feel. For anyone who doesn't have an innate passion for writing, the craft can seem quite daunting and difficult. Yet, telling your story is too valuable to leave it unwritten. The last thing you want is regret not having written it. It is for this reason that I've created this simple journal and workbook. It's designed to help you take action and get your story on to the blank page. Whatever your purpose is for writing it, this book gets you on the road to achieving your goal.

Thank you for inspiring me. I hope you enjoy using the book, as much as I have had creating it.

Cheers!

Thank You!

There are many people I would like to thank for supporting my journey as a ghostwriter and writing this book.

- First and foremost my mom, Gloria and Uncle Don. Both of you have been my rock and voice of reason. I thank you so much for standing behind me with your generous support and love.

- To John Felstead, I can't thank you enough for being there for me. I am beyond words for all that you've done when you didn't have to.

- Success Circle: Jennifer, Lois and Rhonda. We have had an awesome journey for more than five years, sharing our career dreams and aspirations. I feel so blessed to know you. Thank you so much for your support.

- My graphic designer, Lillian Jia. I know how crazy it can be with the demands of university, but you maintained such enthusiasm taking on this project. Kudos to you! I wish you all the best for a very bright future.

- Matt Hoffman, you are such a talent. I love your simple drawings. There's so much purity to them and that is why they are in the book. You are going far, my young one.

- To my colleague, turned friend, Sarah Beatty-Russell. You have a lot to do with this book. Thanks for helping me work through some of my creative blocks. Never doubt your creative genius, my dear!

- To my new love, Wayne Brown, who provided me the space and freedom to follow my calling. I thank you so much for your encouragement and unconditional love.

...Last but not least, to Francesca Davino, Heather Morosin, Renu Sharma, Olga Sousa-Dias, Howard Davidson and LaRue Shields, thank you for your feedback and input into the content of the book. Your willingness to help and support me is truly appreciated.

Before You Begin...

Often I'm asked what I mean by *story* when it pertains to this book. I usually respond by saying any story you feel the impulse to write: your passion, history, poetry, song lyrics or novel. We know there are many different types of stories for our entertainment and learning. Just to name a few: memoirs, thrillers, short stories - both fiction and non-fiction - journalistic and personal experience stories.

I also say story, because stories have a way of healing us. I've been amazed at the transformation in people's lives, because they found the courage to express what mattered to them. Stories have the ability to clear up misunderstandings, reveal what we've been unconsciously hiding from ourselves and express our truth. Moreover, stories are the thread that connects us to each other as human beings. We are able to relate, learn, grow and be inspired by others' experiences. Stories exist in the smallest daily observances or in the grandest sagas that play out in the world around us. They have a way of keeping us grounded in our humanness and make us remember that we are far more capable, resilient, courageous and endearing than we realize.

In a **Psychology Today** article, it stated that stories are the most effective form of human communication – more powerful than any other form of packaging information.

So I say write what inspires you and feel the need to express. It could be about your whole life or the most exquisite portion(s) you want remembered. Or you may wish to turn a painful time in your life into a novel.

What This Book Is Not

Passion to Paper is meant to help you take the first steps to write your story. It does not engage in the 'mechanics' or 'language' of writing: grammar and punctuation usage, character or plot development, or different styles of writing. There are hundreds of books and courses available that will help you with those things. This book's purpose is to get the story off your chest, so to speak. It may be used as the prerequisite to taking classes if you are so inclined, because you have a story you can hone and make better.

Hopefully, **Passion to Paper** will make you feel more comfortable, familiar and excited about the world of writing.

Tools You Need

The beauty of writing is that it isn't an expensive craft. When Rubin Carter, who I had the privilege of knowing, wrote his bestselling memoir: *Hurricane: The Miraculous Journey of Rubin Carter,* he was incarcerated for a crime he didn't commit in the 60's. He was locked in solitary confinement for a large percentage of his 25 years in prison. He started writing his story on toilet paper, with a small stick of pencil!

For this workbook, you will need the following:

1. **A computer**—have certain tools at your disposal to make writing your story a little less stressful, such as grammar and spell check. Another helpful feature is if you delete and change your mind, you can undo the deletion. Not that simple if you threw your work in the trash can!

2. **A typewriter** – *what*? I know...who uses a typewriter these days? But it may help you channel one of the great authors of old. It may keep you in the mood to write.

3. **Writing pads, pens and pencils** – for the moments when sitting in front of a computer is tiresome. Computers drain energy and can affect our ability to stay focused and think clearly. Tuck a small notepad in your pocket, take a walk and write in long-hand for awhile. You will be surprised by the flow of information that comes through your hand on to the paper. We have become addicted to the conveniences of electronic devices, but the practice of writing helps to stimulate our brain and creative energy.

   Inspiration comes in flashes and when you least expect it. You don't want to lose those nuggets of insights.

4. **An open mind** – the exercises provided in the book have been used time and again and come from personal and professional experience. They will get you moving forward. Trust me. Please keep an open mind. You'll be surprised!

I wish you the best of luck and cheers to you for embarking on this journey. I invite you to stay in touch and let me know how you are doing by becoming a member of the Passion to Paper community: www.passiontopaper.ca/storycircles. You will also find tips and inspirations to keep you going.

"Every man's work, whether it is literature or music or pictures or architecture or anything else, is always a portrait of himself."~ Samuel Butler, 19th Century English Author and Artist

This book belongs to:

Name: _____

Project (I am working on or would like to work on.)

Date: _____

"There are thousands of thoughts lying within a man that he does not know till he takes up the pen and writes." ~
William Makepeace Thackeray
Author of ***Vanity Fair***

Table of Contents

The Power of I AM

I truly believe that we came into this world to find out who we really are. Whether we want to admit it or not, we are writers and each one of us has a story to tell. It is important and valuable to write our stories.

I've noticed in today's society that people like to leave themselves out of the equation when they are speaking. They describe themselves by "you" instead of "I". I know this sounds rather strange, but what I'm referring to is using the "I am" statement when we are talking, because when we say these words, they empower us to grow and fulfill our potential.

Life is a lovely tapestry of humankind and our stories make it colorful and dynamic.

I'm currently working on writing my memoir at 76 years old and I'm finding it very inspirational. It is showing me my capacity to survive cancer three times and two marriages. I've unleashed my artistic and creative abilities to thrive in my contentment for what I was, what I am and what I am becoming.

Pauline Winkle
Painter, Published Author and Poet

"Nobody has a clue, despite all the expertise, what the world will look like in five years, let alone in 2065. The unpredictability is staggering."
~ Sir Ken Robinson, Creativity Expert

Foreword

I have had the pleasure of working with Sherree for a number of years in the world of corporate communication. Together we've seen the good, the bad and the ugly, and are still able to laugh about it all.

In 2009, I was delighted to hear that she was leaving that world to start her own business as a freelance ghostwriter. Much of what she did included partnering with people who wanted to write their own personal stories. This turned out to be a great fit for Sherree, as she has knack for capturing what a person wants to say, in her or his own 'voice.'

Passion to Paper is a natural evolution in her career. Her step-by-step guide helps people make the journey themselves, providing them with the tools and inspiration to bring their own creativity to the page in whatever prose or poetic format they choose. Sections at the end of the book address presentation, printing and publishing options.

If you are interested in discovering your own creative voice through the act of writing, and experiencing the joy it brings, I highly recommend this book. Following the exercises will enable what is unique about you to bubble up to the surface as you discover and hone your own writing style. It is truly a journey of transformation.

Creative Strategist and Writer

Part 1

Understanding My Creative Process

"I believe that what we want to write wants to be written. I believe that as I have an impulse to create, the something I want to create has an impulse to want to be born. My job is show up on the page and let that something move through me. In a sense, what wants to be written is none of my business."~ Julia Cameron, Author of ***The Right to Write***

Sometimes when we are given the privilege of birthing an idea, we are often confronted with challenges we never expected. We can easily identify some of the obvious ones: inexperience, fear of the unknown or the mundane hick-ups that typically occur when bringing a project into fruition. What if the challenges are not related to those obvious things? Instead they are our own internal mechanisms that we didn't relate to until this moment. For example, the internal critic that tells us we are overstepping our boundaries, because we don't have a writer's bone in our body!

Before you begin writing your story, it's best that you have a better understanding of your own creative process, especially if writing is a new journey. One of the biggest misconceptions about writing is the assumption that all we have to do is sit at the computer or desk and our thoughts will flow on to the page like a stream of consciousness, and it will be written exactly the way we imagine it. Not exactly true! Unfortunately, for some of us when we realize that it is a diligent process that takes time and careful work, we grow impatient and frustrated, and we put our story on hold – sometimes permanently.

As famed author, Joseph Heller said, ***"Every writer I know has trouble writing."***

It's comforting to know that we are not alone. Great writers experience one challenge or another with the craft. However, they understand their own creative process; they understand what they need to do to keep moving towards the finish line.

This section of the book is an important step to get your story written. It deals with understanding how your own creative process works and the kinds of challenges or obstacles that often stand in your way. By completing the exercises outlined on the following pages, you will be able to harness your creative power and competently handle the challenges that may arise by being able to see them for what they are and move your story forward.

Important: Please <u>Do Not</u> skip any of the exercises in this section of the workbook! Each one has a purpose and all will reveal itself in the end.

"The path of self-expression is a journey
to self-discovery and self-love."

Please write in the space below the challenges you are facing or believe will be of concern when you begin your project. For example, a very busy schedule, no support from friends or family. Not enough knowledge on the topic. Be honest and keep writing until you think you have everything down on paper.

Challenges:

What's *Really* Holding Me Back?

Now, here comes the interesting part: what if there isn't anything standing in your way, except you? Picture this: You are sitting in front of your computer, staring at a blank page. You need to start: *How do I begin?* You write a couple of sentences... delete! Try again... "Once upon a time"...delete! Let's try again... "Jill opened the front door; Jerry is standing there... *What will Jerry say?* Oh boy...delete! You leave the computer and go to the refrigerator...maybe a snack will help. *You know... this refrigerator hasn't been cleaned in a while. Geez, I haven't spoken to Sadie in a while....I'll give her a call.*

What about having self-doubt? *What made me think I can do this?*

Write in the space below the diversions you use to avoid starting or finishing your story.

"Sometimes, one just has to shut up, sit down and write." ~ Natalie Goldberg, Author of ***Writing Down the Bones: Freeing the Writer Within***

Getting to the Hear t of the Matter

Sometimes procrastination or self-doubt is the root of something else.

This exercise is to get to the heart of the matter. It requires cold, hard honesty.

1. When I think about my story, I am (exhilarated, honored, vulnerable...)

2. When I start writing, I am (happy, focused, overwhelmed...)

3. When I feel blocked or unable to keep the momentum going, I become (frustrated, tired, anxious, wanting to move to another project...)

4. **When someone criticizes me for my efforts, how does it affect me? (I become disheartened; I rise to meet the challenge...)**

5. **From the words or phrases written above, write below the ones that most resonate for you.**

Feeling Exercise:

If I am completely free to write, how would it feel? (It is very important to get in touch with the *feeling:* **Describe the feeling (excited, happy, scared...)**

* How you *feel* is the key to manifesting your story.

"...the art of creation is not entirely a
rational and conscious one." ~
Salman Rushdie, Author of
The Satanic Verses

Sharing Exercise: To have others' support you is invaluable. For this exercise, ask someone or people you trust to share their own solutions with you. Write them below.

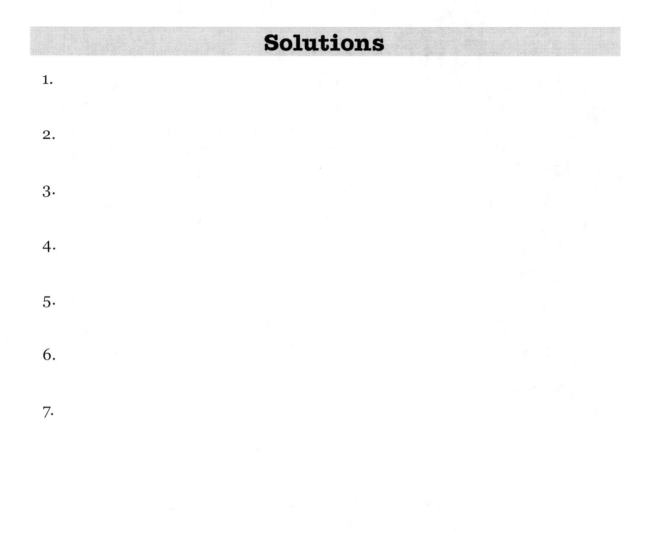

Solutions

1.

2.

3.

4.

5.

6.

7.

"I value my time. I choose to use it wisely and do not let others steal it from me." ~
Paula E. Coxed, Author, **Finding Time**

Getting in Touch with My Creative Expression

Having discipline is an important prerequisite to manifesting anything we want to create. But discipline has been labeled a bad word. Often it is Interpreted as rigid, linear and not fun! Remember that whatever we want to write should come from joy and gratitude.

One way to maintain discipline is to be in the flow of our own innate nature. It's easier to be committed to something when we know how best we operate. For example, if you enjoy the quietude of the early mornings, or late at night, then more than likely you will be up and energized to write and it *feels natural* for you. It's also important to know how you react when obstacles present themselves, because in an instant, you can throw your discipline out the window.

Exercise: The following questions should help you understand how you operate creatively.

1. **When is my best time of day to be creative?**

2. **What do I normally do with my best time of day?**

3. **What prompts or motivates me to be in the 'zone' (totally focused and able to tune out the world)?**

4. **When I'm feeling tired, stressed or unmotivated, how do I bounce back to keep going?**

5. **When spurts of inspiration come, how do I respond to them (act quickly, mull them over, don't do any thing)?**

6. **Who do I admire the most for their creative discipline and success?**

7. **What ideas or philosophy can I take from them and imbibe?**

"Most of us are about as eager to be changed as we were to be born, and go through our changes in a similar state of shock." ~ James Baldwin, American Author

Internal Power

The urge to create something – whether it is a story or another endeavor – we actually *co-create* with our internal power. We can call this power our creative muse, higher/divine-self or intuition This internal power is at our disposal at any time. However, we sometimes block it, because we believe we are solely responsible for our creation. In essence, our mind and ego trips us up by becoming attached to a certain approach, thinking or outcome. What was supposed to be free-flowing and pleasurable becomes writer's block or inertia. We start doubting what we began and become frustrated...angry...or disappointed. Many great writers or artists have said they consider themselves to be the 'conduit' to a creative force that operates outside their ego or mind. It is their job to listen and pay attention to this force.

When approaching your story, consider being in *partnership* with your internal power. Guided by it, it leads you to think outside the box, generate new ideas and keeps you energized and motivated. By the end of the journey, not only are you replete, but amazed at the end result of your creation. Another way to look at this concept is to use the analogy of a bird soaring in the sky. When the bird first lifts off from the branch of a tree, he has to flap his wings with self effort. This self effort is us taking action. But once he's in the air, he doesn't have to flap his wings anymore, because he catches hold of a current of wind and begins to soar and float without effort. The current of wind represents our internal power in grace.

Tapping into this internal power requires spending time in quietude and be willing to hear what it has to say. In this exercise, you are going to write a letter to this power, asking for guidance. Because this power lies within, you will address the letter to yourself. For example, *Dear John or Sue,* if that is your name. Another very important point to consider: the question or statement you pose should be short and succinct to produce the best results. Long-winded statements lose their effectiveness and can be quite frustrating to articulate. Remember, your internal power knows you very well. Also, it instigated the desire or need to write your story, so it knows what you want. You. Just. Have. To. Be. Direct! Here is an example of a simple, direct question: *How do I stay motivated and energized?* Or, *What inspires me?*

After you have written your question or statement, close your eyes and take a few deep, long breaths. Feel centered within your body and just wait for the answer to come. Don't force it. You don't have to do anything, but write what comes up. Do not censor or judge. Very important! Just write freely. Keep writing until you feel there's nothing more to say. Read what you wrote. What stands out or resonates for you? Usually, we are surprised by what we've written — something that we would never have thought of with our conscious, rational mind. This is a good sign, because it means that you gave your internal power the opportunity to speak.

You can use this exercise for any issue or situation when you are looking for clarity. Begin writing...

Letter to Self™

Dear (write your name), _____

> *"Today I do affirm that I am divinely guided...There is
> "That" within which knows what to do and how
> to do it, and It compels me to act on what It knows."*
> ~ Ernest Holmes, Author of ***Science of the Mind***

Letter to Self ™ Cont'd

"And by the way, everything in life is writable about if you have the outgoing guts to do it, and the imagination to improvise. The worst enemy to creativity is self-doubt." ~ Poet and Writer, Sylvia Plath

What Inspires Me?

Finding inspiration is vital to our creative process. To think that we can write without spending time nourishing our spirit and creative self is to deprive our project of its fullest potential. As famous filmmaker Alfred Hitchcock said, ***"Ideas are everywhere."***

With this exercise, think of all the things that inspire you. It could be a favorite movie you watch over and again, your children's playful wonder, a stroll in the neighborhood park or reading a book in a café.

1. _____

2. _____

3. _____

4. _____

5. _____

6. _____

7. _____

"Invent your world. Surround yourself with people, colour, sounds and work that nourish you." ~
Sark, Author of ***Make Your Creative Dreams Real: A Plan for Procrastinators, Perfectionists...***

Creating a Contract

In this exercise, you are going to create a **LETTER OF AGREEMENT** with yourself. This Agreement is a commitment to your discipline as a new and enlightened writer of your story. You are going to take the words or sentence that most resonate for you from each question in the Discipline exercise, What Inspires Me? And from the *Letter to Self* ™.

Write them here:

_____

_____

_____

_____

_____

_____

Place them in the letter on the next page. Print a copy or copies of the letter and put them in places where you can see them often.

*"Whatever you can do or dream you can, begin it;
boldness has genius power and magic in it."* ~
Johann Wolfgang Von Goethe, 18ᵗʰ Century
German Poet, Playwright and Novelist

LETTER OF AGREEMENT

Date

Name

Dear

Congratulations! You have successfully entered into an agreement with your story!

To ensure your journey is a successful and fulfilling one, it is important that you adhere to the terms set out in this Agreement:

1. You will be disciplined according to the way you operate. This involves:

    _____

    _____

2. You accept the fact that you are a co-creator of your story and will adhere to the insight(s) you received from *Letter to Self* ™ It is, or they are:

    _____

    _____

3. You promise to have fun, enjoy the journey, make sure you take care of yourself and embrace what inspires you.

Upon signing, you are committing to the terms stated above.

Please print:_____ Signature:_____

"Your own words are the bricks and mortar of the dreams you want to realize. Your words are the greatest power you have. The words you choose and use establish the life you experience." ~ Sonia Choquette, Author and Spiritual Teacher

Part II

Writing My Story

"Put it before them briefly so they will read it, clearly so they will appreciate it, picturesquely so they will remember it, and above all, accurately so they will be guided by its light." Joseph Pulitzer

Having Purpose and Vision

You've completed Part I. Congratulations! I hope the exercises unleashed surprising information about you that you weren't aware of before.

Before we begin the heart of this workbook, let's take a look at why, or your purpose of writing and your vision.

Purpose ignites the fire that sets you in motion. Whatever you want to create has to have purpose. What is the purpose for writing your story? Is it to leave a legacy for your family and friends? Test your writing mettle? A calling that won't allow you to rest until it is expressed? Publish and share a life-altering experience with the world?

A vision is also important. Holding a vision for the outcome of your creation makes it happen. However, there is an addendum to this statement: *you cannot be attached to the final outcome of your story.*

The following exercise helps clarify why you want to create and starts you on the journey to making it happen.

1. Write below the purpose of your story. For example: To heal old wounds.

"Make visible what, without you, might perhaps never have been seen." ~ Robert Bresson, French Film Director

2. **Visualization Exercise**: You are being honored for your story at a gala for new authors. You are standing on a grand stage in front of a large audience and you are about to give an acceptance speech for winning first place. What would you say about your journey to that moment of achievement? Write it out as if it were your speech.

"Be passionate about what you write, believe in your ability to convey timeless ideas, and let no one tell you what you're capable of." ~ Christina Westover

What Makes a Good Story?

You've set a clear intention for your story and have a vision. Let's talk a little bit about what makes a good story. Each person has their own opinion of what a good story is. The best response to this question would be that a good story is memorable. It creates an emotional connection or response in the reader. For example, the story puts a smile on your face each time you remember it, because of its use of humor. Or it left you feeling encouraged, because it described in detail the main character's journey from extreme adversity to prosperity - something you can relate to.

On the following page, write in bullet form what was it you loved about five stories you read or saw in films - what was it you liked the most in each one?

For example, was it the style in which it was told? The character or characters you loved? What was it about them? What feelings were stirred after reading or seeing the story: encouraged... hopeful... joyful...disheartened...sorrowful?

"The world is made up of stories, not atoms."
~ Muriel Rukeyser, American Poet

Five of My Favorite Books and/or Films

Story #1

Story #2

Story #3

Story #4

Story #5

Keeping in mind what you have written about the stories that are memorable for you, let's briefly look at what great writers or storytellers consider when they are creating their story. Usually, they begin by asking themselves certain questions. Now it is your turn. Your answers will provide perspective and focus. Please answer them as succinctly as you can. They may even surprise you!

1. Who will read your story: Family members?   Children?   A specific target group? Knowing your audience is very important, because having them in mind as you write will keep you connected to them. For example, you will consider the words you use so they don't misunderstand what you are saying.

2. What feelings or emotions would you like your story to draw out in your reader? Compassion? Relief? Understanding? Forgiveness? Empowerment? Courage?

3. What is the overall message you want to leave with your readers after they've read it? For example, your ancestors were tremendous survivors and the genes of strength and courage lies within your children: or your children can be or do anything they want, if they love themselves.

"After nourishment, shelter and companionship, stories are the thing we need most in the world." ~ Philip Pullman

Action Plan (What Needs to be Done)

Having an action plan for your story not only keeps you focused, but most important, the plan shows that you are taking measurable steps towards achieving your goal. Seeing your efforts on paper is very empowering and keeps you moving forward.

Here is an example:
Goal: By December 2014, have my story published.

Steps	Activity	Results of Activity	Follow-up action	Date Done
Step 1	Research the worlds of publishing: self publish? Or traditional publishing?	I will need to go the traditional route	Find a publisher who publishes my book's topic	Saturday, May 1
Step 2	Research Publishers	Found two: Random House & Simon Shuster	Must submit through a literary agent	Monday, May 3
Step 3	Research literary agents	Found one who takes new authors	Contacted agent. Arranged a meeting	Friday, May 7
Step 4	Have manuscript thoroughly edited	Contacted editor to do final edit	Submitted manuscript	Tuesday May 11

"Action is character."~ F. Scott Fitzgerald,
American author of ***The Great Gatsby***

Exercise: Begin by writing your goal. Make sure there is a date to achieve it by and that the date is achievable. Then, in the blank template, write the steps you anticipate taking to complete your story.

Action Plan

Goal: By _____, I _____

_____

Steps	Activity	Results of Activity	Follow-up action	Date Done
Step 1				
Step 2				
Step 3				
Step 4				
Step 5				
Step 6				
Step 7				
Step 8				
Step 9				
Step 10				

"It is good to have an end to journey towards; but it is the journey that matters in the end." ~ Ursula K. Le Guin, American science and fiction writer

Don't Sweat the Details

As a professional writer, I've worked with corporate and individual clients on a variety of subjects. Each one has provided me with the opportunity to grow as a writer and expand my knowledge through their topic of expertise.

One common trait I've experienced with some clients is their sweating the details to the point of not completing their writing or running late on important deadlines. Ultimately, frustration sets in on both our parts; I'm paid off for what I helped start. Some projects die a sudden death. There usually is a promise of picking up the project at some point later, but rarely that ever happens.

One particular client I vividly remember. She is a renowned child psychologist. I felt what she had to share was very enlightening and I was honored to be part of her book.

What began as a collaborative relationship, with both of us working together to develop the book outline, turned into an unhealthy obsession on her part. She started sweating the details while we were trying to complete the first draft of her manuscript. Important deadlines she wanted to meet were not met. The challenge on my part was getting her to stop focusing on punctuation and constant rewriting of a sentence and get her notes and ideas on to the page first. The details will be addressed later. Unfortunately, our relationship abruptly ended and I have no idea if her book was finally written with the help of another writer. I always want to wish my clients the very best, even if our collaboration wasn't successful.

I have worked with others like her and the sad part is their dream to share their experience and knowledge with the world isn't fulfilled.

So, if there is one piece of advice I'd like to give new writers: don't sweat the details, especially when you are just starting. Just get the information on paper and fix it after.

Laura Jones
Professional Writer

"We tend to focus on the annoying expectation... it's helpful to step back and see the bigger picture..."
~ Author Richard Carlson, **Don't Sweat the Small Stuff...And It's All Small Stuff**

A Story's Anatomy

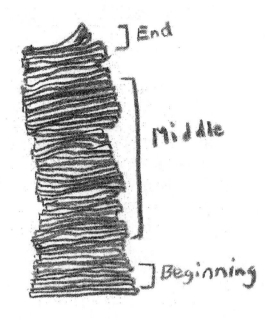

You've created an action plan. Now comes the task of actually writing the story. Where do you start? **Start where you are**. Don't feel the need to begin at the very beginning: *"Once upon a time"..."* *"It began when I was five years old"*, unless you have the impulse to start there. Sometimes starting at the beginning leaves us stuck emotionally. Wherever there is the inclination to start, start there. It could be, *"On travelling through northern Africa I met a medicine man, who became my husband..."* What's important is to begin. Remember that the creative process is organic. Although the process of writing is steady and consistent, *what* you write and *when*, should be spontaneous. The content can be rearranged later.

Exercise: To get you started, you are going to develop the anatomy of your story: the beginning, the middle and the end. But first, write below the theme and the title of the story. Sometimes you'll change the title a few times as you progress along. For now, write what you have in mind.

Story's Theme and Title:

_____

_____

*"A story should have a beginning, middle, and an end...
but not necessarily in that order."* ~
Jean Luc Godard

The Beginning

Where do you want to start your story? You could say that the beginning is giving your story the first breath of life. It's your starting point. Remember, it doesn't always have to begin with, *Once upon a time...or when I was five years old*. It could be, for example: *"As I stood in line to board the plane, it hit me that I would be leaving behind the safety and comfort of everything that is familiar. I've never been on a plane before, let alone to Paris. When I land in Paris, I'll be catching a connecting flight to Iraq."*

Below, write the beginning of the story in bullet form. Once you've written everything you could possibly think of for the beginning of the story, you can weave the points into sentences on your computer or a writing pad.

"The act of writing is the act of discovering what you believe." ~ Sir David Hare, British Playwright

The Middle

The middle is considered to be the heart or backbone of the story. List again here in point form, what you consider to be the story's main message. For example, *"I've been in Iraq for two months and became fast friends with a young sergeant by the name of Jeremy. He took me into the bowels of the combat zone...early one morning in the distance we heard gunfire..."*

"The pages are still blank, but there is a miraculous feeling of the words being there, written in invisible ink and clamouring to become visible." ~ Vladimir Nabakov

The End

Your story's end is where it naturally takes its final breath. Again, write below in bullet points or short sentences what you want to say. Let's continue with the example: *"I'm finally heading home, after spending the most terrifying six months in Iraq and losing Jeremy to a bullet to his chest. My life has profoundly changed. I won't be taking life for granted any more..."*

"Writing is a way of talking without being interrupted."
~ Jules Renard's ***Journal*** (10 April 1895)

Framing My Story

You have finally put your story down on paper. It may not be in its perfect final form, but what's important is it's written. Halleluiah!!!

When we talk about framing your story, we mean putting it in the form of a book by incorporating elements that are common in most books. So let's determine that the Second Draft of your story is putting it into book form. As you know, a book has the following basic elements: an introduction, acknowledgements, chapters, an epilogue or conclusion.

This exercise will help you take the content of your story and frame it. It will also help you see if there are any missing pieces that could make your story more complete.

Acknowledgements: Who do you want to thank and dedicate the book to?
Your children...parents...best friends... colleagues, all of them? Write a sentence or two for each person you would like to thank. Have fun with it!

*"I even shower with my pen, in case any ideas
drip out of the waterhead."* ~ Graycie Harmon

Introduction: This short paragraph introduces the story to your readers. You set the stage for the time or place of the story, introduce the main characters or share your thoughts on why you are writing it. What is your introduction? Write it below.

Chapters: Does your story require chapters? Instead of one long narrative, breaking the content into segments may help the reader follow the story in a clear and succinct manner. Go through your story and see where it could be broken up into segments. Once you have determined what they are, give each segment a title. Write the titles below and number each one as a chapter.

Epilogue: The epilogue is a short passage that is added after the story ends. It concludes the story. It could be a short description of your experience writing it or what has since happened to the main characters. It may even set the stage for another story you will write in the future. You could potentially have a series of stories on your hands. The epilogue is not always necessary. If you don't feel inclined to write one that is perfectly fine.

Part III

What's Next?

*"Write your first draft with your heart.
Re-write with your head." ~ **Finding Forrester***

Review and Edit Your Story

You did it! You've put your story down on paper: wrote your beginning, middle and end; you've added an introduction, acknowledgements, chapters, and if you wanted, an epilogue. Now what?

Now it's time to review and edit what you've written. The following exercises will help you go through your story objectively. Your ultimate goal is to have it flow cohesively and read coherently. What you don't want is to leave your readers confused, guessing or asking, *"What are you trying to say exactly?"* Sometimes, novice writers make the assumption that their readers will understand what they mean. This isn't true. What we are thinking and feeling or even saying doesn't always translate the same way when we are writing. Always think of your readers! Here goes...

1. **Print a copy and read it out loud to yourself.** Why? Because reading out loud provides a different perspective. It also helps you to see some obvious things you may not otherwise catch: spelling errors, gaps in the story or sentences that could be restructured. As you read, try and listen to what you are saying with an objective ear. How does it sound? Is it making sense? Write on the following page your impressions of reading it out aloud. Next, how does it make you *feel* to hear it? Excited...accomplished...sad? Are some of the feelings you are experiencing the same as the ones you want your readers to have?

   - Spelling mistakes are simple enough to correct with the help of a dictionary, hiring an editor or using the spelling and grammar function on your computer.

   - Gaps in the story could be a series of events that are missing or more detail is required about the characters or people. On the following page, write in bullet form the pieces you think are needed to make the story more fluid and complete.

   - What if there are no gaps? All the information is there, but somehow it isn't flowing cohesively. Maybe some parts of the story have to be repositioned. Let's have a little fun. Take a pair of scissors and cut the story into segments. You be the judge of where the cuts should be. Start rearranging the pieces to see how best the story flows. You may find you are reorganizing the pieces a number of times until the story finally resonate well for you.

*"Proofread carefully to see if you any
words out."* ~ Author Unknown

Additional Information Required

Implement the changes you've discovered in the previous exercise and save your document as Draft 3.

2. **Share the story with someone you trust.** You may not be ready to share your story with a wide audience, but one person you trust and value their feedback can make a difference. They will be able to review it with a fresh pair of eyes and perspective. You have been intimately involved with your story and it's been in your heart and head for quite some time before you decided to put it 'out there.' Objectivity is important. For some of us, the idea of sharing makes us feel exposed or vulnerable. We are afraid of being laughed at or receiving negative comments. However, having the best story possible is the ultimate goal. You may be pleasantly surprised by that person's reaction. Don't underestimate the power of your story! If you are afraid of someone close to you looking at it, then ask a teacher, a colleague, a professional writer or editor.

    *   It would be helpful to the person if you specify what you want them to look for. For instance, do you want them to correct grammar and punctuation? Sentence structure or check the story's flow and cohesiveness? Or maybe you only want their overall impression? Let them know what you want and what your goal is for the story.

You've received their comments. Was the feedback constructive and valuable? Are you feeling inspired and encouraged to move forward? Congratulations and implement the suggestions you received. Name your revised story Draft 4 and move on to the next section.

But...

...What if the feedback left you feeling angry or disheartened? Before making any drastic decisions, such as throwing the story in the bottom of a desk drawer or in the trash, leave it alone for a little while, maybe for a few days or a week (not for too long, because you will find all kinds of reasons not to start again), then try the following suggestions to rekindle your enthusiasm to move forward.

*   **Get a second opinion**. If by chance the second person says basically the same thing as the first one, then try to take the feedback graciously and see it as an opportunity to create an even better story.

*   **Go back to Part I: *Getting to the Heart of the Matter*** and remind yourself of how you react when you receive negative feedback. Do you need to make a shift in your perspective and face the challenge?

- **Consider this story the foundation to build on a new one.** The essence of the story is already there, but somewhere it went off track or it needs to be articulated in a different way. Write another *Letter to Self* ™ and ask, *"Please show me the new direction of my story."* Write on the following page what arose for you.

When you are ready, begin rewriting.

Letter to Self™

Dear (Your name)_____:

Presentation

Your story is ready. It feels good to have it finished and you are happy with the end result. Take some time to relish in this great achievement. What will you do? Celebrate with some friends? Or, just enjoy the moment and move on?

You are now at an important juncture of your story's evolution. In this segment we will discuss presentation. Some of the information may seem obvious and elementary, but you would be surprised to know that presentation is often overlooked by many writers.

Whether your goal is to offer the story to family and friends, or decide to publish it, how it is presented makes all the difference. Remember the old saying, *"Don't judge a book by its cover?"* Well...unfortunately, in the world of books and publishing, people do.

There are so many services and options available to make your story look polished so there shouldn't be any reason why the end result couldn't be pleasing to the eye and a treasure for the recipients to accept. Your readers will be very impressed and value what you've done even more.

Here are some tips to give your story a wonderful, professional look without breaking the bank:

- If your goal is to have it published and sold in the marketplace, it is *highly* recommended that you have a professional editor look at it, even before you take it to a publisher. It is worth the investment. It's also helpful if the editor is familiar with the genre of your story. They will certainly know what to look for with their editorial eye. If money is an issue, a copy editing student at your local university or college can be of help.

- Hire a graphic designer to design the layout of your text. Depending on your story, you want it to be pleasing for the readers' eyes. If it is a book of poetry or text-only novel, it may not be necessary. A graphic designer will suggest the type and size of the font, break up the text and add photographs or illustrations here or there. They will also know how the text should be laid-out for typesetting and printing purposes. Again, if you are on a tight budget, a graphic design student from a Community or Graphic Arts College can do it for you. Your project will help build their portfolio.

- If a graphic designer is not an option and you want to keep your story as simple as possible, your local printer can help. Most of them provide additional services such as basic formatting, printing and binding the copies you need at a minimal cost.

- Add images, if the story warrants it. Imagery draws the eyes away from the text and allows them to rest. Images also help anchor your story, because they visually bring the words to life. They could be family photographs or illustrations.

Other Options:
Print on Demand

If the idea of seeking individual services seems daunting, time consuming and expensive, there are many online bookmaking services and tools cropping up on the Internet that take the hassle and stress out of publishing on your own. Their basic service allows you to upload your story and images into a preformatted book layout and they will print the number of copies you want. They also provide additional services at extra costs: professional editing, graphic design, typesetting; printing, marketing and distribution services. They will also sell your book on their online bookstores.

Many of these online companies are called, Print on Demand or POD. Instead of using the traditional method of printing thousands of copies of your story and storing them in your garage until you can sell them, or give them away, you print only what you need. They provide bookmaking software that you can download on to your computer and then upload the content. Usually, the software provides specific guidelines to ensure that when the story is printed it looks professional. For example, photos of the highest resolution or quality can only be used, if you want the end result to look sharp and clear. If the images are not at a high enough resolution, the software will reject them.

You also get to choose whether or not you want the book in soft or hard cover, the quality paper (standard or premium) and the book's size. You are still responsible for ensuring the text is spell-checked and there are certain limitations on how you position the photos within the text. However, this is all for a good reason: the software knows what is required for your story to print out properly in book form.

Once you are ready, you are able to order the number of copies you want and pay for those copies plus shipping and handling. When I first ordered a book I wrote for a client, I was very pleased with the suggestion to order only one copy first to ensure there were no issues with the layout or flow of the story. I did just that, and when it arrived, I was pleased with the end result! It was a beautiful hard-cover book, with four-color images throughout. My client was happy too.

The beauty about online POD companies is that they not only educate, but you can participate in their online community to have discussions with like-minded writers while providing all the necessary tools to publish your story.

In the *Resource Section* at the back of the book, I will list a few POD companies. Some of them you may already know.

Open Sources

If you want to be adventuresome and create your story from start to finish, the Internet provides an array of community-based desk-top publishing software and tools for free. For a person who is not technically adept and has no desk-top publishing experience, the learning curve may be daunting.

> *"My aim is to put down on paper what I see and what I feel in the best and simplest way."* ~ Ernest Hemingway

Part IV

Taking My Story to Market

*"In matters of truth the fact that you don't want to
publish something is, nine times out of ten,
a proof that you ought to publish it."*
~ British Author, Gilbert K. Chesterton

The Publishing World: An Over view

This segment of the book provides a general overview about the world of publishing, if your goal is to take is to take your story to market. The following information has been garnered from personal experience, countless hours of research and discussions. It's important to note that the publishing world is constantly evolving, so use the information as a stepping stone to make an informed decision about your own project.*

In recent years, the world of publishing has been going through tremendous change. With the advent of the Internet and digital printing, both are making it more economical and easier for *anyone* to publish. There are more choices available than ever before and this is exciting news.

With new emerging choices available, the big question is which route to take? Let's have a look...

* New and updated information will be posted on **Passion to Paper** website: www.passiontopaper.ca.

"If there's a book you really want to read, but it hasn't been written yet, then you must write it." ~
American Author, Toni Morrison

Traditional Route

When we speak of the traditional route of publishing, we are referring to publishing houses with which an author submits their story based on certain criteria of the publisher. When a publisher accepts the manuscript, the author has a professional team to:

- Distribute the story to bookstores and other sales channels

- Make the story available in other countries and languages

- Consult on book cover design and title

- Send out review copies

- Purchase advertising and promote the story to booksellers and libraries

- Copy-edit and typeset

- Print copies

In essence, they assume all the responsibility and upfront costs to get your story into the marketplace. In return, they take a large percentage of the book's sales.

A traditional publisher's business model involves an author submitting a well-written query letter or book proposal, detailing why they think their book is worth publishing. It is in the author's best interest to provide information in the proposal or query letter based upon the publisher's submission guidelines to avoid getting a rejection letter.

New authors often find it difficult to get their work noticed by this method. Quite a few will tell you they received numerous rejection letters before a publisher recognized the merits of their story. It takes a lot of perseverance and trust to keep going. Now, another option for authors is to hire a literary agent to represent them. Some of the larger well-established publishing houses will not look at an author's manuscript without an agent. The benefit of having an agent is he or she provides inside knowledge about the publishing industry and helps to sell the merits of your story better than you could do on your own. The downside to this option is finding someone who is reputable and will not make false promises and cannot deliver the desired outcome. Highly reputable ones usually have their hands full with established authors and may not take on new clients.

Within the past decade or so, the traditional publishers' role as gatekeepers for authors has dramatically changed. If we were to have a fireside chat with a few seasoned publishing experts and authors, they would foretell a bleak future for traditional publishing houses that operate under the old business model. In fact, some have stated that many of them will go out of business - unless they adapt and embrace the changing landscape in the industry. Fortunately, some of them are.

It has also been noted that most large traditional publishing houses are primarily focused on publishing books that are guaranteed to be lucrative for them. Either they support the seasoned well-known authors or only consider manuscripts written by political or entertainment celebrities. However, we've all witnessed a few exceptions: JK Rowling *Harry Potter* series or Stephanie Meyers' *Twilight* sagas, or *Marley and Me* by John Grogan. There are many more examples, but these three are well known.

There is definitely a need for publishers. Not all authors – new or seasoned – want to take on the responsibility of trying to publish on their own. Publishers create more value for them than they can do for themselves.

Points to Consider

- Publishers have the experience and knowledge to get your story published and on the shelves of bookstores.

- They have the know-how to improve your story to make it more marketable.

- They usually buy the rights to your story.

- Keep in mind a publisher may do a considerable amount of revisions to your manuscript, because their intention is to make sure it sells.

- Newer publishing houses are recognizing the merits of publishing your story in electronic format (ebooks) so that it reaches audiences who are embracing new media. Barnes and Noble's Nook, Apple's iPad and Amazon's Kindle are Just a few examples of electronic devices that readers are using.

- You are paid an advance.

- Do your research and only target publishers interested in publishing your story's genre. To contact every publisher will not only frustrate them, but also you as well.

- Follow their submission guidelines to a tee. If you don't, it will certainly guarantee a rejection letter. Most publishers will post their guidelines on their website or you can visit your local library or bookstore and look through the *Writers' Market* handbook. For more information on what is involved in writing a query letter or book proposal, you can contact your local Association of Publishers.

Self-publishing Route

As the old saying goes, *"when one door closes, another one opens"*. If you've tried the traditional route and can't seem to make head-way with publishers, take heart, the door to self-publishing opened large and wide, with unlimited opportunities for any author to publish their own story. However, without a clear understanding of this avenue, it can feel overwhelming and complicated.

Self-publishing means the author has control of his or her own story. Not only are they responsible for writing, but also all the duties a publisher would carry out on their behalf:

- Copy editing

- Book design

- Printing

- Marketing and distribution

Seems like quite a bit to do and finance, but the good news is, more profit goes into the author's pocket, after any initial costs to professionally prepare the manuscript for the marketplace.

Although self-publishing has been around for quite some time (my introduction to the notion of self-publishing was the *Celestine Prophecy*. Boy, that's aging me!), in the past few years, the scales seemed to have tipped more in favour of authors taking the self-publishing route. Even seasoned authors are touting this option and some are by-passing their publisher to take control of marketing and distributing their book.

With the advent of the Internet and digital media, there are many ways to get your story out there; however, figuring out the best way to find fans of your book requires a strategy. The idea of uploading your book on to an online bookstore or to your own website or blog, for example, may not be enough, unless that is all you want. So the important questions to ask are: what's the goal for my book? What do I hope to accomplish?

I've provided web links at the back of the book to do your own investigating and research to make an informed decision. Please note that there are many online self-publishers, such as Balboa Press. On the **Passion to Paper** website, I will provide ongoing updates on the publishing world and the new and emerging services available.

Points to Consider

- You are in the driver's seat of getting your book out in the marketplace, which means more money in your own pocket!

- There are many online retailers that will help your book reach a much wider audience than you could possibly do on your own. However, you have to be proactive in drawing traffic to your book on the sites. Having a marketing strategy that involves social media, such as Twitter, YouTube or a blog and personal interaction with your potential readers are very important.

- Although more and more publishing experts and authors are favoring the self-publishing route, it is still a fairly new and emerging arena from the standpoint of finding aggregated statistics on where to find readership, the length of time it takes to get noticed and how to eventually get the book on to a bookshelf.

- For those of you unfamiliar with digital media and the Internet, self-publishing may be challenging. There's a lot to learn first, but if you are up for the challenge, there are all kinds of online courses, tools, and self-publishers and literary agents willing to help. Do as much research as you can to determine, if this route is right for you.

- Most self-published books do not reach bookstore shelves. If they do, it takes a while. It's definitely not an overnight process. However, it has also been noted that authors who self-publish, and there is a demand for their story, a traditional publisher will offer a book deal. This is the ideal dream of any author!

The Dream

I remember the morning I woke up from a very beautiful, vivid dream. I had it shortly before the economic meltdown in September 2008. In it, a friend and I were shopping in an old warehouse, looking for bargain toys for her children for Christmas. Something made me go to the window in the warehouse and look up into the sky. I saw an angel descending from heaven to earth. My friend and I ran to a small courtyard where she arrived to speak to a crowd gathering around her. She was beautifully adorned with a crown on her head and wore a shimmering white robe and her skin was glowing with radiance. She smiled at us and only spoke these words, "We are in for hard times, but it's not the end of the world..." She kept repeating them over and over again. Behind her a host of other angels descended and they too began repeating her words whilst walking among the crowd in the courtyard. What was profound about the other angels were they looked like ordinary people, dressed in everyday clothing from all parts of the world: Italy, India, America, South America, etc. They were no different from earthly human beings.

A few weeks after the dream, I was watching the afternoon news and witnessed the largest stock market crash since the Great Depression! My life was now in flux, because I couldn't find my next assignment in corporate communications after a contract ended with an international company. Phone calls or emails were not being returned from recruiters or companies where I applied for work. This went on for more than a year. I took the odd job here and there just to get by. But remembering the dream became a balm to soothe my anxiety about what to do next. I had to keep reminding myself not to be drawn into fears that the media was perpetuating. I didn't want to buy into it. What good would it do?

I went for long walks and sought solace in nature, prayed and meditated for guidance. Then one day I decided to seek outside help, because I was puzzled by the fact that I was having a hard time finding work, when usually it was fairly easy for me. I went to see a professional astrologer, who is also very intuitive and she and I became friends. Over cups of tea, she looked over my astrology chart and informed me that my days of corporate work were over! And that it was time for me to begin my work as a healer. So I asked the question, what kind of healing work am I to do? I'm not interested in going back to school...again and my talent lies in communications. She agreed and went on to say that my healing work would be through helping people tell their stories.

She continued by saying that people of our generation – specifically boomers – would experience tremendous change and upheaval, because it is time for them to live their lives authentically and let go of what is no longer working. They too will reach out, wondering what to do and you'll help them find clarity.

After our session, I felt uplifted and relieved and began to tie together what she told me with my dream. But first, I finally had to admit to myself that I hated the corporate world and it was time to move on to something new – something that would make me happier and fulfilled. I had to be resolved in my decision to move on and not look back.

So, I began my journey as a ghostwriter, because writing was an essential component of what I did in corporate communications. It was an easy transition in terms of skills, but I had to learn how to make a living – which was challenging to say the least.

It's been four years since I started helping people tell their stories. Has it been easy? No, far from it, primarily because of the misconception many people have about the process of writing. It's been an ongoing learning for me as well as for them. But the calling to do this work has never died.

As I pay close attention to what is going on in the world today, again I'm reminded of the dream. Humanity is going through significant changes and it does feel as though the world is ending. I don't subscribe to fear-mongering, nor do I believe in burying my head in the sand, thinking that everything is alright. When I wake up each morning, I realize that every passing day is one day closer to a world that is transformed into something even more beautiful than what it was before. Those who rise above their own adversities and transform their lives will have the most inspiring stories to tell.

Final Chapter? Hope not!

Will completing your first story be your last? Whether you decide to continue writing and sharing more personal stories, my wish for you is that you enjoy the journey. We learn so much about ourselves, and the more we know about our own modus operandi, the more empowered and compassionate we are towards others. Sharing your story is an act of compassion and generosity.

Your family, friends and readers will certainly appreciate your accomplishment, because the more they know about you, the more they learn about themselves. As I stated, never underestimate the power of your story.

I want to remind you that the exercises outlined at the beginning of the book can be applied to almost any creative endeavor you embark on. When you understand how you operate creatively, you harness the power to fulfill your goals and dreams. Please enjoy using the tools I've provided.

Cheers to you for completing your story! I wish you great success and all the best.

Coming soon: ***Passion to Paper: A recipe for writing your business story.*** Stay tuned!

"The writer writes in order to teach himself, to understand himself, to satisfy himself; the publishing of his ideas, though it brings gratification, is a curious anticlimax." ~
Alfred Kazin, ***Think*** (1963)

Part V

Sticking With It

"Stopping a piece of work just because it's hard, either emotionally or imaginatively, is a bad idea. Sometimes you have to go on when you don't feel like it." ~ Stephen King, American Author

Tips and Words of Wisdom

When you are feeling tired, or can't find the right words, get up, take a walk or stretch. Computers are known to drain our energy. Find another location and write in long-hand for a while.

Drink lots of water and avert your eyes from the computer screen from time-to-time.

Always carry a note book wherever you go. Spurts of inspiration come in a flash and unexpectedly. You want to be prepared to capture them.

"Dance is one of the most powerful forms of magical ritual...It is an outer expression of the inner spirit" ~ Ted Andrews, Author and Teacher

Move the body to keep your energy flowing and your mind alert: take a walk, or turn on some music and dance, do a little housekeeping.

Take a 'power' nap (20 to 30 min) to rest the mind and body. It's amazing how new thoughts and ideas flow freely after.

"We need to give ourselves permission to write 'badly' so many of us would write very well indeed" ~ Julia Cameron, Author of *The Artist's Way*.

Always get your thoughts down on paper without editing. Just let the words flow. Don't worry about order, or grammar. Just write; write until you can't write anymore. Leave it alone and then come back at a later time to review, fill in blanks or add more thoughts. Leave the editing for much later.

Be gentle with yourself.

Make a creative space that is solely your own. Have music, put up photographs, or words of wisdom from your favorite artists. Make the room an inviting place for your creative muse.

"I write what I want to write. I write what amuses me. It's totally myself." ~ J.K. Rowlings, British Author of **Harry Potter** books

What to do When I'm Challenged?

1. Write a *Letter to Self* ™

2. Do what inspires you. It's important to nourish your spirit and creativity.

3. Keep great company. Call a friend who supports your endeavor.

4. Revisit your Action Plan. Maybe you haven't taken a step that is necessary to move you forward.

5. Contact me to guide you and/or join a **Passion to Paper** story circle. It's a collaborative and safe environment to get unstuck or renewed enthusiasm on your story: w w w.passiontopaper/storycircles.ca

Suggested Readings

Keep company with the experts through reading their books. They provide inspiration, information and encouragement. There are many books on creativity and writing. The ones below are my favorites, which I keep close at hand.

Julia Cameron

- *The Artist Way*
- *The Right to Write*
- *The Vein of Gold – A Journey to Your Creative Heart*

Stephen K ing

- *On Writing: A Memoir of the Craft*

Stephen Pressfield

- *The War of Art: Break Through the Blocks and Win Your Inner Creative Battles*

> *"We can do anything we want to do if we stick to it long enough."* ~ Helen Keller, deaf and dumb wrote her biography, ***The Story of My Life***

Publishing Resources

Writer's Market Handbook

WMH is a great handbook for writers who want more information about publishing their story. It lists publishers in different genres and what they are looking for from writers. It's updated every year. You can also join The Writer's Market online community for a small fee: www.writermarket.com and receive updates, and participate in various courses, conferences and webinars to improve your writing.

There are many traditional and self-publishing services available. Here are a few online self-publishers you can consider.

Blurb.com or Blurb.ca

Whether you want to print and publish your story in hard copy or as an ebook, they provide all kinds of services to help new authors publish books; especially those who want to give books as gifts for family and friends. They also will help you sell your story.

Lulu.com

Like Blurb, Lulu provides similar services.

Amazon's CreateSpace – www.amazon.com

Provides self-publishing services and access to a wide distribution network. Kindle is Amazon's digital device for downloading ebooks, including your story if you choose to publish electronically: www.kdp.amazon.ca or .com

Barnes & Noble NookPress – www.nookpress.com

Book Baby – www.bookbaby.com

Kobo Writing Life – www.kobo.com/writinglife

The choices are endless! Please do your own research to make the right decision for you.

Please use the following pages to express: sketch, jot ideas or write sparks of insights.

"A word is a bud attempting to become a twig. How can one not dream while writing? It is the pen which dreams. The blank page gives the right to dream."
~ Gaston Bachelard French philosopher and poet

Self-Expressions

"We do not learn by experience, but by our capacity to experience." ~ Lord BUDDHA

Self-Expressions

"A hunch is creativity trying to tell you something."
~ Frank Capra, American Film Director

Self-Expressions

"Jump" ~ Joseph Campbell, American
writer, mythologist and lecturer

Self-Expressions

About the Author

Sherree Felstead began her career in corporate communications more than 20 years ago. She has worked for global companies and three levels of government in Canada, helping senior management and employees orchestrate and write internal and external communications. She has also directed and produced award winning presentations.

Since leaving the corporate world in 2009, Sherree has worked as a ghostwriter, partnering with first-time authors to write their inspirational books, personal stories, and web content.

Passion to Paper is a reflection of her own personal journey as a writer, meditation practitioner and teacher for those wanting to write about their passion for the first time.

"I've approached this book from the standpoint that writing is an internal journey into one's own nature. The craft has a way of bringing up aspects of ourselves that we don't often pay attention to or notice, because most of us focus on the external. With writing, we are mostly alone with it and that can be overwhelming.

"I want to show people that yes, it's not easy, but they are not alone. Most of the great writers felt the same way and persevered. To persevere is to awaken a beautiful and noble virtue."